High-Tech Sports

capstone
classroom

BTR Zone (Bridge to Reading) is published by Capstone Classroom,
1710 Roe Crest Drive, North Mankato, Minnesota 56003
www.capstoneclassroom.com

Copyright © 2014 by Capstone Classroom, a division of Capstone. All rights reserved. No part of this publication may be reproduced in whole or in part, or stored in a retrieval system, or transmitted in any form or by any means, electronic, mechanical, photocopying, recording, or otherwise, without written permission of the publisher.

ISBN: 978-1-62521-110-1 (paperback)

Editorial Credits
Adrian Vigliano, editor; Eric Manske, designer; Eric Gohl, media researcher

Photo Credits
Alamy: Oliver Furrer, 55; AP Photo: Amy E. Powers, 25, Daily Inter Lake/Brenda Ahearn, cover, John Zeedick, 31; Corbis: 26, Hall of Electrical History Foundation/Schenectady Museum, 16; Courtesy of Sportvision: 13, 23; CriaImages.com: Jay Robert Nash Collection, 6; Dreamstime: Rob Corbett, 45, Ronald Callaghan, 46; Getty Images: Allsport Hulton, 36, Andy Devlin, 42, Collegiate Images, 34, John Giamundo, 41, Transcendental Graphics/Mark Rucker, 58; Library of Congress: 8, 19, 32; Newscom: Cal Sport Media/Chris Szagola, 12, Cal Sport Media/Randy Sartin, 14, ZUMA Press/Dan Krauss, 39; Science Source: Ted Kinsman, 21 (top); Shutterstock: Action Sports Photography, 4, Aspen Photo, 21 (bottom), Denis Pepin, 10, Eric Broder Van Dyke, 24, Greg Epperson, 51, Haslam Photography, 57, LouLouPhotos, 28, Maridav, 59 (bottom), Max Earey, 52, Maxim Blinkov, 59 (top), Richard Paul Kane, 11, Vince Clements, 48

Design Elements: Shutterstock

About the Cover
Elijah Pitts of the Green Bay Packers runs with the ball against the Kansas City Chiefs during Super Bowl I.

Printed in the United States of America in North Mankato, Minnesota.
032013   007223CGF13

TABLE OF CONTENTS

CHAPTER 1
Sports Tech 5

CHAPTER 2
Baseball Tech 17

CHAPTER 3
Basketball Tech......................... 27

CHAPTER 4
Hockey Tech 37

CHAPTER 5
Extreme Sports......................... 49

Great Sports Firsts.................... 58
Read More............................... 60
Internet Sites 60
Glossary of Text Features 61
Glossary................................. 62
Index..................................... 64

Better helmets have changed the way football is played.

CHAPTER 1

Sports Tech

A 260-pound (118-kilogram) **linebacker** sprints across the field. He throws his whole body forward to make a dramatic tackle. As he crashes into the other player, both players' helmets **collide**. Both players crumple to the ground and lie still. The crowd is shocked into silence. After a few tense seconds, the players get to their feet and jog to opposite sidelines. They are OK!

Without their protective helmets, these players could have suffered serious injuries from such a hard hit to their heads. But thanks to improving technology, football players and other athletes are now better able to avoid injuries. In addition to improving equipment and uniforms, technology has also influenced certain rules and training methods. Because of improvements in sports technology, athletes of all kinds can perform at higher levels. They face fewer risks of serious injury.

linebacker · a defensive football player
collide · to crash into

Football Helmets

Even though football players are often big and strong, it is against the rules for them to play without **helmets**. There have been many advances to football helmets over the years.

The first football helmets were made of leather.

When football first started in the late 1800s, helmets were made of leather. They didn't have much padding, and they were not very protective. Many football players of this time period suffered serious head injuries, and some even died. The invention of plastic helmets with padding inside greatly reduced the number of head injuries. Football helmets have been made of plastic since the 1950s but continue to improve in other ways.

The first plastic helmets did not have **face guards**. A face guard is a metal frame attached to the front of a helmet. This piece protects a player's face from injury. Now all football players wear helmets with face guards. Some modern players add **visors** to their helmet. A visor helps a player see better in the glare of the sun or stadium lights. Another major advance in football helmets was the addition of radio devices. With a radio-equipped helmet, a player can hear plays called in from his coach while the player is on the field.

helmet · protective head covering worn by an athlete

face guard · metal guard that attaches to a helmet to protect the face

visor · a clear or tinted piece of plastic on a helmet, used to protect the eyes

Protective Gear

Football players have also changed since the beginning of the sport. During the last century they have gotten bigger and more athletic. Years ago it was not unusual for a player to be 180 pounds (82 kg). Today players often weigh more than 300 pounds (136 kg). As players became larger and stronger, they needed better equipment to protect themselves.

Early football players wore far fewer pads than today's players do.

Protective gear, such as shoulder pads, thigh pads, and braces, have gone through several improvements. Early football players wore pads made of leather. These didn't offer much protection. Plastic and foam pads were used in the 1960s. These were more protective, but they also held in body heat. Players could overheat in this kind of gear.

In 2002 lightweight fibers designed for astronauts were used to make football gear. This gear allowed air to pass in and out more freely, and players did not overheat. The University of Florida in Gainesville even designed personal air-conditioning systems to cool down players. When players were on the sideline, they could hook up to an air pump. The pump blew cool air through their pads.

The Football

The football is the "oddball" in the world of sports. Most other major sports use a round ball. The football has an interesting history that led to its unusual shape.

The rough English sport of **rugby** led to what is now known as American football. Like rugby, football in the 1800s used running and kicking plays. The first football looked a lot like a rugby ball. It was made from an inflated pig's **bladder** and was the shape of a watermelon. This is why a football is sometimes called a "pigskin." When rubber was invented in the mid-1800s, it replaced the pig's bladder. Eventually, leather was used to cover the rubber to make the football stronger and easier to handle.

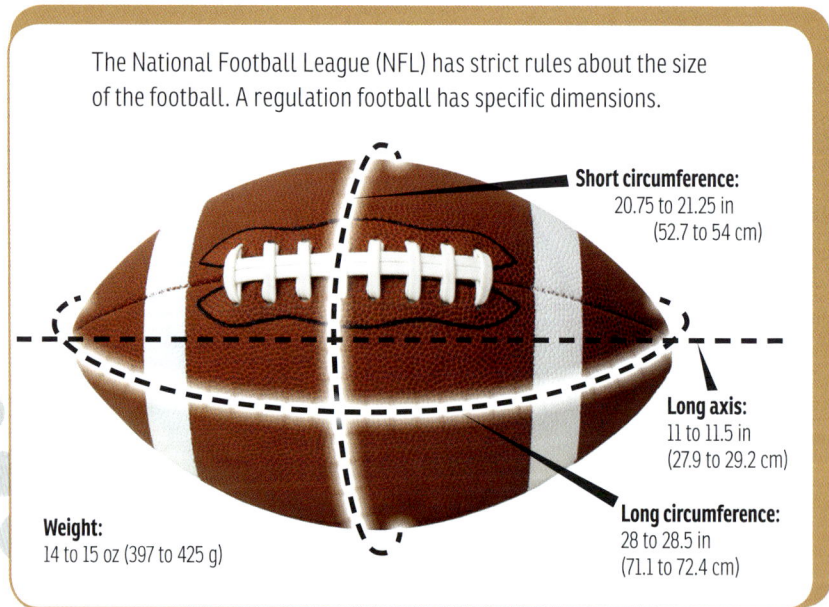

The National Football League (NFL) has strict rules about the size of the football. A regulation football has specific dimensions.

Short circumference:
20.75 to 21.25 in
(52.7 to 54 cm)

Long axis:
11 to 11.5 in
(27.9 to 29.2 cm)

Long circumference:
28 to 28.5 in
(71.1 to 72.4 cm)

Weight:
14 to 15 oz (397 to 425 g)

Forward passes had a huge impact on the development of football.

The football changed again when the **forward pass** became a legal play. The first forward pass was thrown on September 5, 1906, during a college game. As the forward pass became popular, the football's shape needed to change. Players needed a ball that could move through the air more smoothly. The shape of the football had to become more **aerodynamic**. The more narrow-ended shape of a modern football allows players to throw it longer distances and with greater accuracy.

rugby • sport that inspired football

bladder • organ that is a part of the urinary system

forward pass • pass thrown in the direction that the offensive team is moving

aerodynamic • design of objects to help them move through the air faster

Camera Technology

It is near the end of the game, and the score is tied. A player makes a fantastic catch close to the goal line. But a referee signals "no catch." He says the player was out of bounds. The crowd thinks it's a terrible call, and people begin booing.

Referees make sure athletes follow the rules. They used to rely only on their judgment, and their judgment was based on what they saw. The NFL now uses camera technology to help referees make correct rulings. A coach can throw a red flag on the field to protest certain rulings. The referees review the replays from multiple angles and speeds to determine what actually happened.

The review has several steps. First the play is shown several times, using instant-replay technology. The action is shown in slow motion. It is even reviewed in freeze-frame technology. This process shows each moment of the play in a still image. After watching all of these, the referee knows for sure what the right call is.

An NFL referee watches a replay to make sure the ruling on the field is accurate.

The Yellow Line

TV networks use computer technology to highlight the first down with a yellow line. This line helps fans watching on television keep track of the game.

yellow line

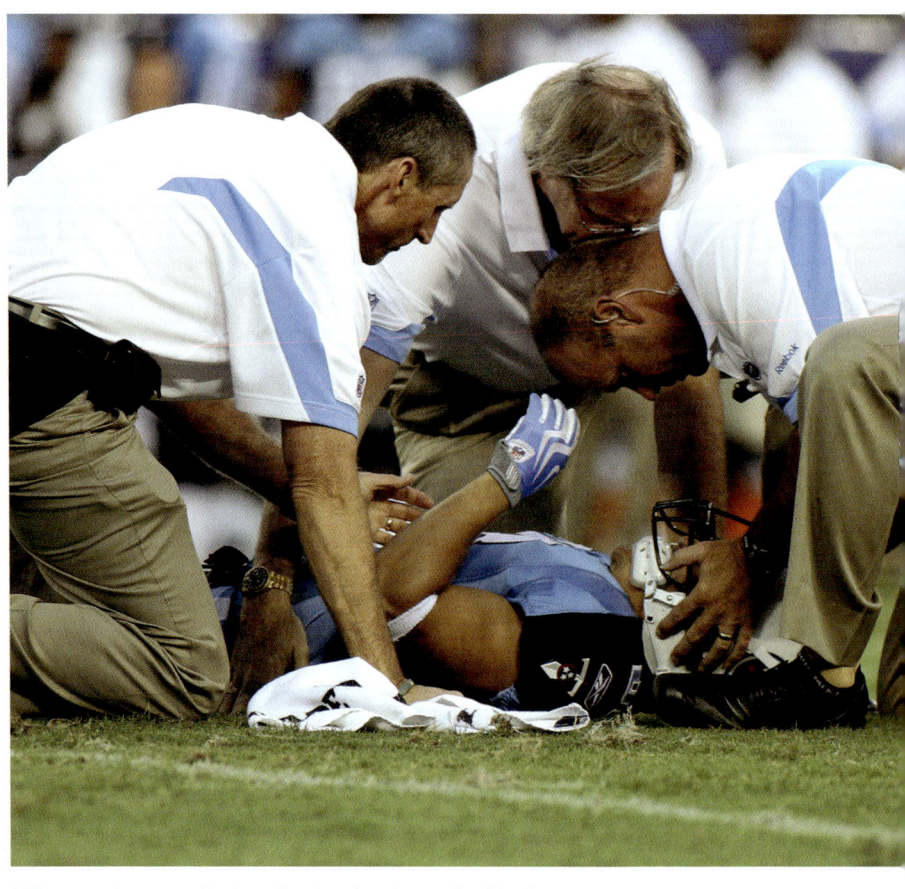

NFL teams have medical professionals who work with players.

Diagnosing Injury

Many football teams have doctors on the sidelines in case a player needs medical attention. Injured players can be treated on the sideline or taken directly to an examination room.

Concussions are one of the most serious sports-related injuries. Doctors have developed computerized tests for concussions. One of these tests checks the memory skills of players. Memory loss is a sign of concussion. If a player cannot pass the test, he is kept out of the game. Players used to be sent right back into the game if they seemed OK. Today coaches and medical personnel are better trained to put players' safety first.

Doctors also use high-tech medical scanning devices to help them identify athletes' injuries. These devices can produce three-dimensional images of the brain and muscles. These images make it easier for doctors to see exactly where and how someone is hurt.

concussion · injury to the brain due to jarring from a blow or fall

Night games were a major improvement for professional baseball.

CHAPTER 2

Baseball Tech

It's Electric

On the evening of May 24, 1935, a crowd of 25,000 baseball fans waited anxiously in the stands. The Cincinnati Reds were getting ready to play the Philadelphia Phillies at Cincinnati's Crosley Field. This was no ordinary game. The excited fans expected to see something that had never before taken place in a Major League Baseball game. Major League Baseball is a professional baseball league.

Approximately 400 miles (644 kilometers) away, in Washington, D.C., President Franklin D. Roosevelt was waiting for a signal. When the signal came, he threw a switch. That switch sent a million **watts** of electricity flowing toward Cincinnati. At Crosley Field 632 stadium lights came on, turning evening into daylight. Fans were about to watch the first nighttime Major League Baseball game.

In the 1930s and 1940s most stadiums installed lights. More and more games were held at night. The use of electricity would forever change the sports world.

watt · unit used to measure power

Evolution of Baseball

Electric lights instantly changed the sport of baseball. Fans loved attending night games, and they became very popular. However, not all technological advances in sports happen so suddenly. Most advances occur over long periods of time. Baseball as we know it today was played basically the same way 100 years ago. But the equipment that baseball players use has gone through some improvements.

The Glove

In the 1800s baseball players wore unpadded work gloves made of leather. Sometimes they wore no gloves at all. In 1885 **shortstop** Arthur Irwin added padding to his glove. He was trying to protect two broken fingers. After this more players started adding padding to their gloves. By 1900 all players wore padded gloves. **Catchers** were allowed to wear larger gloves and face masks to help protect them behind home plate.

---

shortstop · baseball position that covers the infield between second and third base

catcher · baseball player stationed behind home plate

Early padded gloves helped protect players' hands.

The Ball

The first baseballs were much smaller and lighter than the ones used today. By the late 1800s, baseballs started to resemble modern balls, which have rubber-coated corks in the centers. Over the cork are layers of yarn. String is wound tightly over the yarn. Then the whole ball is covered with pieces of leather held together with exactly 108 hand-sewn stitches. An official baseball weighs between 5 and 5 ¼ ounces (between 142 and 149 grams).

The Bat

Early in baseball history, there were no rules about bat size or weight. Players experimented with bats made of different woods. Some players tried bats that were flat on one side. Most players found that a round shape worked best. In the 1920s players started using **aluminum** bats. These lightweight bats allowed hitters to make faster, stronger swings. Most baseball leagues, except the major leagues, use aluminum bats today.

Bat Controversy

Because aluminum bats can be swung faster and hit a ball harder, they pose a safety risk to players. Some people think aluminum bats should be banned to protect the safety of **amateur** players.

Inside of a Baseball

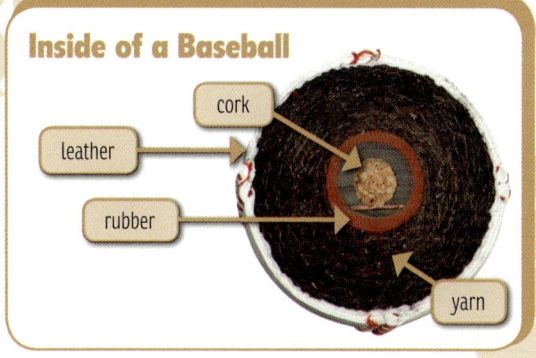

A college player swings an aluminum bat at a pitch.

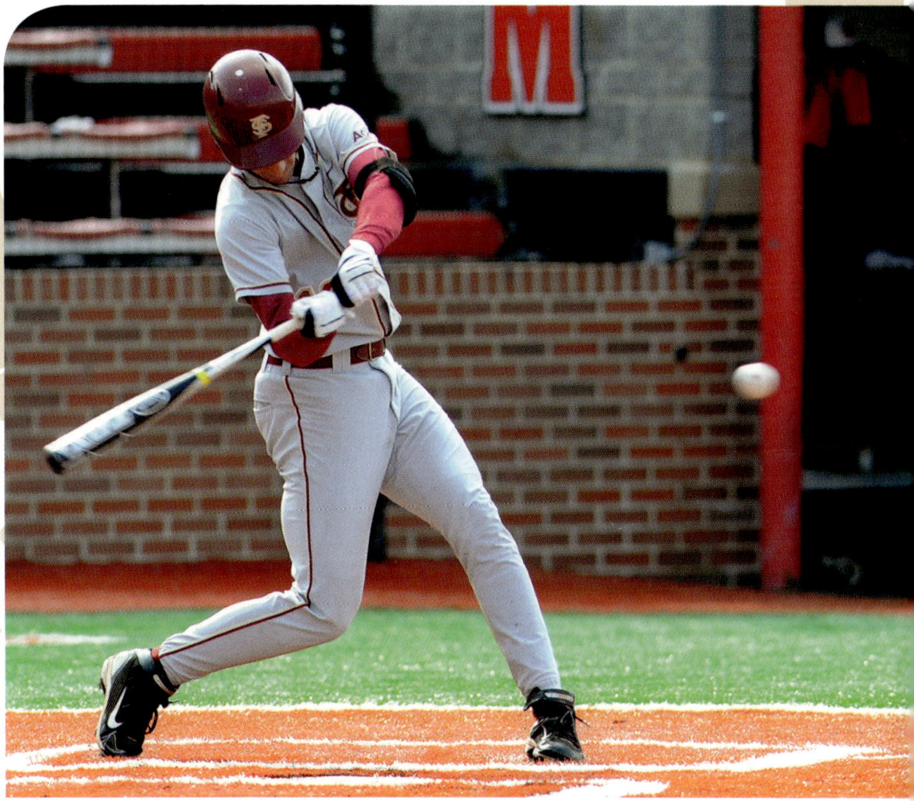

aluminum · a silver-white metallic element

amateur · an athlete who does not compete for a payment

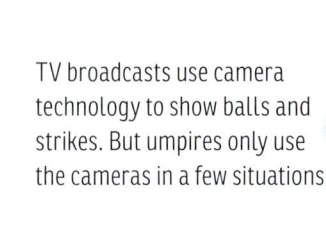

TV broadcasts use camera technology to show balls and strikes. But umpires only use the cameras in a few situations.

Electronic Eye

In professional baseball, umpires make decisions on every play. They decide, for example, if a runner is out or if a ball was caught. According to the current rules, umpires can use instant-replay technology in only three situations, all involving home runs:

- **Home-run call**: Did the ball land above the home-run line or go over the fence?
- **Fair or foul**: Was a ball that appeared to be a home run in **fair** or **foul** territory?
- **Fan interference**: Did a fan interfere with the flight of the ball?

fair · when a ball is in play
foul · when a ball is out of play

Many people think technology should be used more often to make baseball decisions. One way to add more technology would be to replace human umpires with camera technology to make these decisions. Many people think using such technology would honor the spirit of baseball. The decisions would be right every time.

But many other people like having human umpires. They feel that replacing umpires with camera technology would ruin a baseball tradition. Some people think umpires should make easy calls but rely on technology for close calls.

Artificial Turf

In 1966 Major League Baseball first used **artificial turf** instead of natural grass. Officials thought the fake grass would cost less to maintain. They also thought the artificially smooth field would help fielders by reducing the number of bad ball bounces. But fielders discovered that artificial turf also caused them problems. On the plastic grass, hard-hit **ground balls** were more likely to skip by a player's glove. The same ground ball on natural grass would move more slowly and be easier to catch.

Only two remaining professional baseball fields use artificial turf.

Part of this artificial turf is made from a mixture of sand and recycled rubber.

Some argue that artificial turf is fair for both teams because it is always the same. Natural-grass fields can be different from one stadium to another. For example higher grass could cause ground balls to move more slowly. But many people think these differences add to the fun of baseball games. Today only two Major League Baseball teams still use artificial turf in their stadiums.

artificial turf · plastic ground covering that looks like grass

ground ball · a ball rolling on the grass

High school basketball players prepare for a jump ball in 1899.

CHAPTER 3

Basketball Tech

At a school gym two teams **dribble** and pass a ball for several minutes. After a long time one of the players finally shoots and scores. The ball drops into a wooden peach basket nailed to the wall, 10 feet (3 meters) off the ground. The game is stopped so a referee can climb a ladder to get the ball.

The previous scene describes what basketball was like when it started in the 1890s. As the sport became more popular, the bottoms of the peach baskets were cut out so the ball would drop through. Peach baskets were replaced with iron hoops. Eventually nets were added to the iron hoops.

Early Basketball

The first recorded game of basketball took place in 1892. William Chase made the winning basket with a 25-foot (8-meter) shot. The final score was 1–0! Back then, the game moved much slower than it does today. Players mostly dribbled and passed the ball and rarely made shots.

dribble · to bounce a basketball

Shot Clock

The score is 19–18. There are two minutes left on the clock. The team with the lead is just standing in place. Its players are passing the ball back and forth to one another. They aren't even trying to shoot. If they can keep the ball away from the other team, the remaining seconds will tick away, and they will win.

The shot clock helps make basketball games fast and exciting.

This strategy required discipline and practice to keep the ball away from the other team. But many people found the strategy boring and against the spirit of the game. That's why the shot-clock rule was added in the 1950s. The shot clock gives men's college teams 35 seconds to shoot the ball, and women's college teams get 30 seconds. In the National Basketball Association (NBA), the team with the ball has 24 seconds to take a shot. The NBA is a professional basketball league. If a team doesn't take a shot during the set time, possession of the ball goes to the other team. Large timers are displayed to help college and pro players decide when they should pass, dribble, or shoot the ball.

Thunder Dunk

During a game in Kansas City in 1979, Darryl Dawkins leaped into the air and made a spectacular **slam dunk**. Dawkins, who was called "Chocolate Thunder," ripped the **rim** out of the Plexiglas **backboard**. The backboard shattered into pieces. Glass went everywhere. Spectators at the game said it sounded like a bomb exploded. Some of the players got small cuts from the flying glass. The game had to be stopped until a new backboard could be installed. Dawkins became known for his thunderous dunks and shattered backboards.

NBA officials realized how dangerous these dunks could be for players, referees, and even fans. Dawkins was told he would be fined the next time he shattered a backboard. The broken backboards prompted the league to install shatterproof backboards with safer rims on every court.

> **slam dunk** · a basketball move when a player jumps in the air and pushes the ball through the net
>
> **rim** · metal ring that the ball is shot into in basketball
>
> **backboard** · part of a basketball net behind the rim

A college player shatters the backboard after a slam dunk.

High Tech Isn't Always Better Tech

Though James Naismith invented the sport of basketball in 1891, the basketball itself wasn't invented until several years later. Early players dribbled and passed a soccer ball around the court. In 1894 the first basketball was made from leather pieces that were laced together.

A college athlete holds a 1920s style basketball.

The basketball has gone through several makeovers since its invention. In the 1940s molded leather was first used to make a new style of basketball. For the next 50 years most basketballs were made this way. In 1992 the first composite leather basketball was developed. Composite leather basketballs were made with a mixture of leather and high-tech materials. These new materials gave the ball a softer touch. This allowed players to have more control of the ball during a game.

The NBA started using high-tech composite balls in 2006. However, players didn't like the way they felt. The NBA switched back to basketballs made of molded leather. High-tech isn't always better tech!

Super Shoes

In the early days of basketball, players wore sneakers made from canvas and rubber. Back then, there weren't many types of shoes to choose from. Most players wore canvas "high-top" shoes. These shoes gave players ankle support. High-top shoes were simple and not very expensive. A lot has changed since then.

College basketball players wore canvas high-top shoes in 1948.

Today basketball shoes come in many colorful designs and can be very expensive. Sneaker companies compete to make a stylish shoe that enhances a player's movements and jumping skills. They also add safety features to help players avoid injuries.

Over the years manufacturers have used many different kinds of technology to make basketball shoes. One type of shoe featured an inflation system. A person wearing the shoe could pump the shoe's tongue to push air into the sides of the sneaker. This gave it a custom fit. Sneakers have evolved with changing technology. Some shoes even have devices that tell a player how high he or she jumped. These shoes also track a player's movements around the court.

Canada's hockey team scores against the United States in the 1924 Winter Olympics.

CHAPTER 4

Hockey Tech

It's a beautiful cold, crisp day. A whole town has gathered around a frozen pond to watch a hockey game. Ice hockey, as it is known today, started in Canada in the 1870s. The game is played on ice between two teams of six players each—five skaters and a goalie. Players score goals by shooting a puck into their opponents' cage using a stick with a wooden blade attached to it. A goalie stands in front of each cage and tries to stop the puck from going in. Ice hockey's rules have changed little since its beginning. However, technology has dramatically changed where and when the game can be played.

Hockey teams used to have to wait until it got cold enough for a pond or lake to freeze in order to play. Today indoor ice rinks can be built any place in the world. Cold weather is not needed to play ice hockey, but you do need the technology to make the ice.

From Frozen Pond to Hockey Rink

In the early 1900s, indoor ice rinks were built in Canada and the United States. The technology used to make an ice floor is similar to a refrigerator, just on a much larger scale. Under the ice are layers of different materials and cooling devices. Workers cool the ice in 12 stages to get the perfect skating surface.

Maintaining a smooth ice surface used to be difficult. Workers had to scrape the ice to remove the nicks caused by skaters. Then they had to spray fresh water on the rink and wait for it to freeze again. The invention of the **Zamboni** in the 1950s changed all that. The Zamboni is a kind of tractor that quickly scrapes the ice and adds water to the rink at the same time. A Zamboni can have an ice rink good as new in minutes.

Today new technology can create **synthetic** ice. Synthetic ice comes in panels that can be connected together. It works like regular ice, except no cooling is required. With synthetic ice, you could ice skate right in your own home.

Some synthetic ice fits together like pieces of a puzzle.

Zamboni · machine that smoothes the surface of the ice on a rink

synthetic · fake

Puck

The first hockey **pucks** were square wooden blocks. A lot has changed since then. Today hockey pucks are round disks made of rubber. They are one inch (2.5 centimeters) thick and three inches (7.6 cm) in **diameter**.

When struck hard by a hockey stick, a puck can fly across the ice at more than 100 miles (161 km) per hour. Because they are so small, hockey pucks can be very hard to see on a TV screen. Even referees and coaches sometimes have a hard time seeing a fast-moving puck. To address this problem, modern pucks are packed with electronics so they glow and be followed by **global positioning system** (**GPS**). This helps referees make correct calls because they can track the puck more easily.

Hearing the Puck

Hockey is a sport enjoyed by many people, even the visually impaired. Engineering students designed a special hockey puck that makes noises as it moves over the ice. Blind hockey players can tell where the puck is by hearing it instead of seeing it.

In the late 1990s electronic pucks were used in games. The technology created a glowing puck on TV screens for at-home viewers.

puck · a black rubber disk that is hit into a goal in hockey

diameter · the width of a circle

global positioning system (GPS) · a device that receives signals from satellites in the sky

Skates

Ice skates have been around for thousands of years. Over time they have gone through many improvements. Early northern Europeans used skates made of bone or wood to move across frozen rivers and lakes. These skates attached to boots with leather straps. Ancient skaters used poles to help them move.

Modern hockey skates are designed for maximum speed and flexibility.

The first ice skate with a blade attached to a boot was created in the 1800s. This made skaters more stable on the ice. Since then hockey skates have gone through many more changes. They now have wider double-edged blades that help skaters move faster. The boots of ice skates are more flexible and lightweight than they used to be. This helps the skater move more like he or she is running on the ice.

Electric Skates

Ice skates are now being developed with heated blades powered by batteries. A heated blade melts the ice as it moves across it. This helps the skater move faster.

Stick

Traditionally, a hockey stick is made of wood. Two pieces of wood are molded together to make the blade and the long handle. Today hockey sticks are sometimes made from a blend of materials. These composite sticks are usually made of **Kevlar** and other materials. The advantage of a composite stick is that it is lighter and more flexible than wood. When a hockey player takes a **slap shot**, a composite stick will bend a little more when it hits the puck. This makes the puck move faster.

During the 1920s, hockey players used sticks of all different lengths. Referees soon discovered that long sticks were a danger to other skaters. A new rule said that all sticks must be 63 inches (160 cm) long or less.

Kevlar · tough material that is bulletproof
slap shot · a fast shot at the goal in hockey

In the 1950s hockey players experimented with bending the blades of their sticks. They found that a curved blade can create an unpredictable slap shot. This could surprise a goalie and help a shooter score. However, the uncontrolled shot could also fly in unsafe directions. A new rule limited how much blades could be bent.

A stick bends slightly during a powerful shot.

blade

Advances in equipment help protect hockey goalies.

Headgear and Face Masks

There are many reasons why protective headgear should be worn while playing hockey. The sport is played on a frozen surface with a high-speed, hard, rubber puck. Players skating with sharp blades and long sticks slam into one another. The National Hockey League (NHL) did not make players wear protective headgear until 1979. The NHL is a professional hockey league.

The first goalie masks and helmets were made of leather. These evolved into plastic and rubber helmets. In 2000 helmets made of Kevlar were first produced. Kevlar is the material used in bulletproof vests. Kevlar makes helmets virtually indestructible. All players in the NHL must now wear helmets.

GPS in Hockey

Coaches can now monitor players' positions and speed on computer screens. They do this with the help of GPS technology and special cameras. Coaches use this information to help them decide who to put in the game for different plays.

A skateboarder balances atop a ramp.

in-line skate · roller skate that has its wheels in one straight line

truck · a metal piece that connects the wheels to a skateboard or roller skate

polyurethane · a tough plastic used to make the wheels on roller skates and skateboards

CHAPTER 5

Extreme Sports

Skating and Skateboarding

Extreme sports have made huge advances since the metal-wheeled roller skates of the 1950s. New technology allowed for the invention of skateboarding and **in-line skating**.

The skateboard was invented by surfers who wanted a fun activity when they weren't in the water. Early skateboards were made with roller-skate wheels attached to a board. These wheels didn't allow skaters much movement. By the 1970s roller skaters and skateboarders were pulling off all kinds of crazy new tricks. This was due to the invention of skateboarding **trucks** and lightweight **polyurethane** wheels.

In the 1980s a new type of roller skate hit the market—the in-line skate. Having the wheels in one straight line allowed skaters to move in new and exciting ways.

Technology is always changing the world of skating. Today, you can go off-road skating on rough surfaces or even ride a remote-controlled electric skateboard.

Rock Climbing

Rock climbers are going places they've never been able to go before. Over the last 50 years, rock-climbing equipment has gotten lighter, stronger, and safer. Climbers are now able to use **carabiners**. These small rings are made of aluminum. They have special mechanisms that are very light but can hold up to 2 tons (1.8 metric tons). Modern climbers also use new kinds of rope made of nylon that can stretch a little. This helps protect climbers from injury if they fall and end up dangling from a rope. Recently, people have been working on developing "gecko gloves." Geckos are small lizards. They are great climbers. Inspired by the feet of the gecko, these gloves would allow climbers to scale a vertical rock, just like a gecko would.

carabiner · a D-shaped ring used for fastening ropes

climbing wall · a wall built with different holds, used to practice rock climbing

hold · a place where a climber can grab a rock and pull himself or herself up

New technology allows climbers to practice their sport in unique ways. Some climbers install **climbing walls** in their homes. The wall can be programmed so that different **holds** light up, creating endless climbing pathways.

A climber holds on with the help of a carabiner.

Surfing

Mention the word *surfing*, and many people will think you're talking about the Internet. But to a growing number of extreme athletes, surfing is a daring sport. It can be enjoyed on water, on snow, and even in the air.

A professional windsurfer competes in Maui, Hawaii.

Water Surfing

It all started on the water. Ancient Hawaiian cultures started the surfing craze. The first surfboards were solid planks of wood. Today's surfboards are made of special, lightweight materials. They are built with fins on the backs to prevent them from sliding sideways.

Some surfers have fun today by riding "air boards." This type of board sits on top of a pole. As the surfer picks up speed, the pole moves through the water and rises up. This lifts the board and the surfer above the surface of the water.

In 1948 American artist and boat builder Newman Darby attached a sail to a board and the sport of windsurfing was born. Today the boards and sails are made from modern materials that are lightweight and don't get heavy when wet.

Snowboarding

People who liked skateboarding and wave surfing were involved in creating and improving the first snowboards. One inventor found inspiration from riding a cafeteria tray down a mountain. Another inventor made a carpet-covered snowboard in his high school wood shop. Today snowboards are lightweight and flexible. They have superslick undersides to help snowboarders pick up speed for higher jumps.

Sky Surfing

The most extreme type of surfing is sky surfing. In sky surfing a two-person team jumps out of an airplane together. The "surfer" uses a thin board strapped to her or his feet to push against the air currents to create different movements. The surfer's partner films the action with a camera on his or her helmet. The footage is watched by judges on the ground who score the pair's artistic moves. After 60 seconds of sky surfing, the teammates pull their parachutes and float to the ground.

One member of a sky-surfing team performs his routine in midair.

Cycling

In the world of extreme biking, there are two types of bikes—mountain and BMX. Mountain bikes are designed to move over rough trails. They have big wheels. They also have special devices to help bikers jump over fallen trees or move over rocky ground. Mountain bikes are built out of lightweight but tough materials. BMX bikes are designed with small wheels so riders can make quick movements on the street or a **half-pipe**. BMX bikes have handlebars that can turn all the way around. They are designed to help riders pull off different kinds of jumps and tricks.

Technology plays a big role in keeping extreme-sports participants safe. Many helmets protect the brain from head-on impacts. **Neuroscientists** have been working with engineers to produce high-tech helmets that also protect the brain from injuries to the side of the head.

Phone App

Smartphones can help extreme-sports athletes improve their skills. A new app measures **hang time** and amount of **rotation**. It then instantly uploads the information to the Web.

A BMX rider performs a vertical trick.

half-pipe · structure used in skating, snowboarding, and biking that resembles the shape of a swimming pool

neuroscientist · doctor who specializes in the brain and nervous system

hang time · amount of time an athlete is in the air during a jump

rotation · the act of turning

Great Sports Firsts

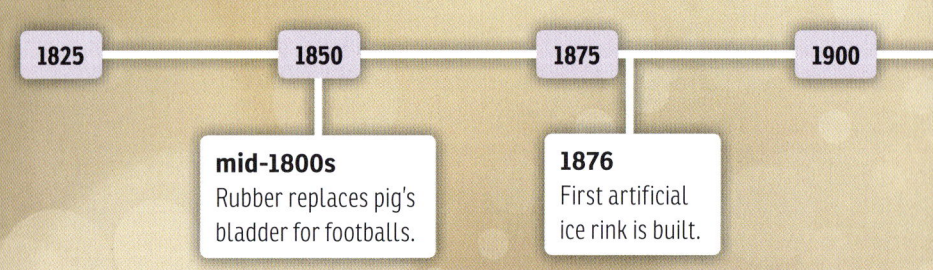

| 1825 | 1850 | 1875 | 1900 |

mid-1800s
Rubber replaces pig's bladder for footballs.

1876
First artificial ice rink is built.

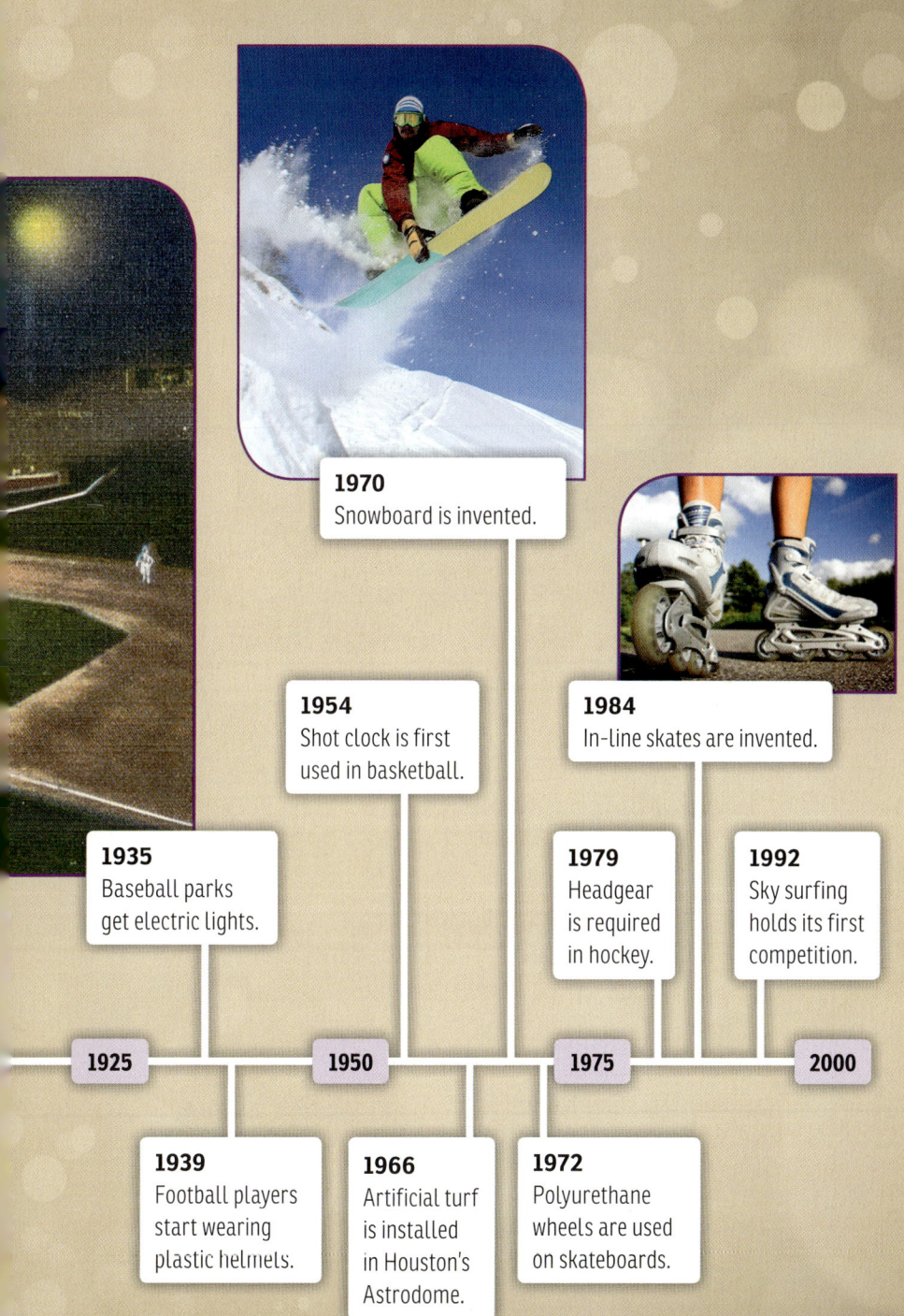

1970
Snowboard is invented.

1954
Shot clock is first used in basketball.

1984
In-line skates are invented.

1935
Baseball parks get electric lights.

1979
Headgear is required in hockey.

1992
Sky surfing holds its first competition.

1925 — 1950 — 1975 — 2000

1939
Football players start wearing plastic helmets.

1966
Artificial turf is installed in Houston's Astrodome.

1972
Polyurethane wheels are used on skateboards.

Read More

Adamson, Thomas K. *The Technology of Baseball.* High-Tech Sports. North Mankato, Minn.: Capstone Press, 2013.

Frederick, Shane. *The Technology of Football.* High-Tech Sports. North Mankato, Minn.: Capstone Press, 2013.

Mason, Paul. *Snowboarding.* Winter Sports. Chicago: Raintree, 2014.

Siemasz, Greg. *Hockey.* Winter Sports. Chicago: Raintree, 2014.

Internet Sites

FactHound offers a safe, fun way to find Internet sites related to this book. All of the sites on FactHound have been researched by our staff.

Here's all you do:
Visit *www.facthound.com*
Type in this code: 9781625211101

Check out projects, games and lots more at
www.capstonekids.com

Glossary of Text Features

Text Feature	How to Use it
Caption: A word or group of words shown with a picture or illustration	Read a caption to understand information that may not be in the text.
Diagram: A drawing that shows or explains something	Examine a diagram to understand steps in a process, how something is made, or the parts of something.
Glossary: List of key terms with their meanings	Look up key terms in the glossary to find their meanings and to get a better understanding of the topic of the text.
Index: Alphabetical list of key terms, names, and topics in a text with their page numbers	Use the index to find pages that contain information you are looking for.
Map: A drawing that represents a place, such as a country or city	Use a map to understand relative locations and determine where events took place.
Photograph or Illustration: Visuals that are created by cameras or drawn	Examine photographs and illustrations to better understand ideas in the text that might be unclear.
Subhead: Word or group of words that divides the text into sections and tells the main idea of a section	Use subheads to locate information in the text and understand how a text is organized.
Table: Represents data in a small space	Examine a table to understand data or to compare information in the text.
Table of Contents: List of the major parts of the book and their page numbers	Use a table of contents to locate general information in the text and see how the topics are organized.
Text Box: A box in the text that provides extra information about a topic	Read a text box to understand interesting or important information.
Text Style: Bold, color, or italic words in the text	Pay attention to bold, italic, and color to figure out which words in the text are important words.
Timeline: Shows events in the order in which they occurred	Use a timeline to understand the order in which events occurred or how one event led to another.

Glossary

aerodynamic (AIR-oh-dahy-nam-ik) • design of objects to help them move through the air faster

aluminum (uh-LOO-muh-nuhm) • a silver-white metallic element

amateur (AM-uh-tur) • an athlete who does not compete for a payment

artificial turf (ar-ti-FISH-uhl TURF) • plastic ground covering that looks like grass

backboard (BAK-bawrd) • part of a basketball net behind the rim

bladder (BLAD-er) • organ that is a part of the urinary system

carabiner (KAR-uh-bee-ner) • a D-shaped ring used for fastening ropes

catcher (KACH-er) • baseball player stationed behind home plate

climbing wall (KLAHYM-ing WAWL) • a wall built with different holds, used to practice rock climbing

collide (kuh-LAHYD) • to crash into

concussion (kuh n-KUHSH-uhn) • injury to the brain due to jarring from a blow or fall

diameter (dahy-AM-i-ter) • the width of a circle

dribble (DRIB-uhl) • to bounce a basketball

face guard (FEYS GAHRD) • metal guard that attaches to a helmet to protect the face

fair (FAIR) • when a ball is in play in sports

forward pass (FAWR-werd PAS) • a pass thrown in the direction that the offensive team is moving

foul (FOUL) • when a ball is out of play in sports

global positioning system (GPS) (GLOH-buhl puh-ZI-shuh-ning SISS-tuhm) • a device that receives signals from satellites in the sky

ground ball (GROUND BAWL) • a baseball that rolls on the ground after being hit

half-pipe (HAF PIPE) • structure used in skating, snowboarding, and biking that resembles the shape of a swimming pool

hang time (HANG TAHYM) · amount of time an athlete is in the air during a jump

helmet (HEL-mit) · protective head covering worn by athletes

hold (HOHLD) · a place where a climber can grab a rock and pull himself or herself up

in-line skate (IN-lahyn SKEYT) · roller skate that has its wheels in one straight line

Kevlar (KEV-lahr) · tough material that is bulletproof

linebacker (LAHYN-bak-er) · a defensive football player

neuroscientist (NOOR-oh-sahy-uhn-tist) · doctor who specializes in the brain and nervous system

polyurethane (pol-ee-YOOR-uh-theyn) · a tough plastic used to make the wheels on roller skates and skateboards

puck (PUHK) · a black rubber disk that is hit into a goal in hockey

rim (RIM) · metal ring that the ball is shot into in basketball

rotation (roh-TEY-shuhn) · the act of turning

rugby (RUHG-bee) · sport that inspired football

shortstop (SHAWRT-stop) · baseball position that covers the infield between second and third base

slam dunk (SLAM DUHNK) · a basketball move when a player jumps in the air and pushes the ball through the net

slap shot (SLAP SHOT) · a fast shot at the goal in hockey

synthetic (sin-THEH-tick) · fake

truck (TRUHK) · a metal piece that connects the wheels to a skateboard or roller skate

visor (VAHY-zer) · a clear or tinted piece of plastic on a helmet, used to protect the eyes

watt (WOT) · unit used to measure power

Index

artificial turf, 24, 25, 59

backboards, 30

climbing walls, 51
cycling, 56

forward passes, 11
freeze-frames, 12

GPS, 40, 41, 47

half-pipes, 56
hang time, 56
helmets, 5, 6, 7, 47, 54, 56, 59

in-line skates, 49, 59

Kevlar, 44, 47

National Basketball Association (NBA), 29, 30, 33
National Football League (NFL), 10, 12, 14
National Hockey League (NHL), 47

polyurethane, 48, 49, 59
pucks, 37, 40, 44, 47

rock climbing, 50, 51
roller skating, 49
rugby, 10

shot clocks, 28, 29, 59
skateboarding, 48, 49, 54, 59
sky surfing, 54, 59
slam dunks, 30, 31
slap shots, 44, 45
slow motion, 12
snowboarding, 54, 57, 59
surfing, 49, 52, 53, 54

trucks, 49

visors, 7

Zambonis, 38